Grammar, Spelling & Vocabulary

Activity Book

Benchmark Education Company
145 Huguenot Street • New Rochelle, NY 10801

Project Editors: Lisa Yelsey and Rose Birnbaum Creative Director: Laurie Berger Art Director: Glenn Davis

Printed in China. 9039/0321/02103-Y29499

ISBN: 978-1-5125-7835-5

Table of Contents

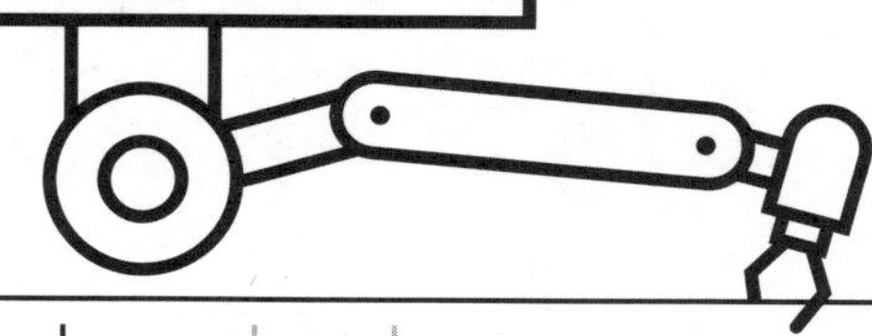

Grammar

Name ______________________ Date ______________

Commas in Greetings and Closings

Letters or e-mails begin with a **greeting**. A greeting includes a word such as **Dear** or **Hi** and the name of the person you are writing to. A comma comes after the greeting. Diary or journal entries may also begin with a greeting.

Dear Mrs. Grant**,** **Hi** Carlos**,** **Dear** Diary**,**

Put a comma in the correct place for each letter opening.

1. Dear Ann
Will you come to my party?

2. Dear Diary
I rode my bike to school.

3. Hi Kelsey
Meet me tomorrow.

4. Dear Teddy
Did you find your gear?

5. Hi Aunt Kay
How are you?

6. Hi Grandma
I miss you.

Read the start of a letter below. Then write it correctly on the lines.

7. Dear Adam Thank you for the gift.

____

____

Name ______________________________ Date ____________________

Commas in Greetings and Closings

Letters or e-mails end with a **closing**. A closing includes words such as **Yours**, **Yours truly**, **Love**, or **Sincerely** followed by a comma. The letter writer's name appears below the closing.

Yours,	**Love,**	**Sincerely,**
Miguel	Mom and Dad	Mr. Chen

Circle whether each group of words is a greeting or a closing. Then write it correctly on the line.

1. Your friend ______________________ greeting closing
2. Dear Eric ______________________ greeting closing
3. Hi Nate ______________________ greeting closing
4. With love ______________________ greeting closing
5. Yours truly ______________________ greeting closing

Read the letter closing below. Then write it correctly on the lines.

6. Your pal Marcus

____

____

Name ________________________________ Date ________________

Collective Nouns

A collective noun names a group of people, places, or things.

A group of . . .	**is called a . . .**
students	class
mountains	range
birds	flock

Underline the collective noun in each sentence.

1. I see a herd of cows.

2. Is that a swarm of bees?

3. The colony of ants makes a hill.

Replace each noun in ( ) with a collective noun from the box that best completes the sentence. Write the collective noun on the line.

crowd	band	team

4. The (musician) plays a tune. ____________________

5. The (person) cheers. ____________________

6. Our favorite (player) wins. ____________________

Name ______________________________ Date ______________

Collective Nouns

A collective noun is singular even though it names more than one. A collective noun is used with a singular verb. A singular verb ends in **s.**

Our **family eats** together.

The **jury listens** to the judge.

The **audience laughs** at the joke.

Underline the collective noun in each sentence. Then rewrite the sentence with the correct form of the verb.

1. Our troop camp outdoors.

____

2. The forest come alive.

____

3. A flock of birds sing.

____

4. A herd of deer graze.

____

5. A school of fish swim.

____

6. A gang of hikers walk past.

____

Name ______________________________ Date ______________

Past Tense Irregular Verbs

Past tense verbs tell about things that have already happened. Past tense verbs that do not end in **-ed** are called irregular verbs. Examples include the following:

Present	**Past**
fall	fell
slide	slid
tell	told
take	took

Choose the correct past tense verb from the box to complete each sentence. Write the verb on the line.

take	told	slide	fell
fall	tell	took	slid

1. Snow ____________________ last night.

2. We ____________________ a walk in the snow.

3. I ____________________ across dangerous ice.

4. I ____________________ Mom about the weather.

Underline the verb in the sentence. Then rewrite the sentence replacing the underlined verb with the past tense form.

5. Many leaves fall. ____________________________

6. I slide down the hill. ____________________________

Name ______________________________ Date ____________________

Past Tense Irregular Verbs

Some past tense verbs do not end in **-ed**. These verbs are called irregular verbs. Examples include the following:

Present	**Past**
hide	hid
throw	threw
dig	dug
grow	grew
see	saw

Choose the correct past tense verb from the box to complete each sentence. Write the verb on the line.

hid	throw	grew	dig
grow	hide	dug	threw

1. My puppy ____________________ big this year.

2. Yesterday, I ____________________ a ball to him.

3. He ____________________ a hole under a bush.

4. He ____________________ the ball in the hole.

Rewrite each sentence using the past tense of the underlined verb.

5. We dig in the sand. ______________________________

6. I see the show. ______________________________

Name ______________________________ Date ____________________

Adjectives

Adjectives tell about a person, place, or thing. Adjectives answer questions such as "How many?" and "Which one?" and "What kind?" For example, they may tell the color, number, or size of an object.

Olga gave me **two** flowers.

She tied them with **pink** ribbon.

She put them in a **small** vase.

Olga is a **kind** friend.

Read each sentence. Circle the noun and underline the adjective.

1. I am a skillful runner.

2. I like to run in cool weather.

3. Will you run one mile with me?

Underline the adjective in each sentence. Then circle whether the adjective describes color, number, or size.

4. There are four kittens in the basket.

Color Number Size

5. The orange kitten is purring.

Color Number Size

Name ______________________________ Date ____________________

Adverbs

Adverbs tell more about an action. They give details about how, when, or where.

We sing **loudly.** We sang this song **before.**

We stand **here.** Our teacher stands **nearby.**

Read each sentence. Circle the verb and underline the adverb.

1. We visited the zoo yesterday.

2. The monkeys played happily.

3. The snakes moved slowly.

4. We watched the penguins later.

5. Mom waited nearby.

Underline the adverb in each sentence. Then circle whether the adverb tells how, when, or where.

6. I always eat lunch.

How When Where

7. Let's eat here!

How When Where

8. I eagerly bite the apple.

How When Where

Name ______________________________ Date ____________________

Contractions

A contraction is a shortened form of a word or words. An apostrophe (') replaces the dropped letter or letters in a contraction.

who is	**who's**
I am	**I'm**
cannot	**can't**
do not	**don't**

Choose the contraction from the box that takes the place of the underlined words. Write the contraction on the line.

I've	couldn't	didn't
won't	she'd	wasn't

1. Dana <u>was not</u> at the game. ____________________

2. She <u>could not</u> get a ticket. ____________________

3. She <u>did not</u> want to stay home. ____________________

4. <u>I have</u> asked her to come over. ____________________

5. She <u>will not</u> come alone. ____________________

6. She said <u>she would</u> bring a friend. ____________________

Name ______________________ Date ______________

Contractions

An apostrophe takes the place of one or more letters in a contraction.

Let us walk to the park.	**Let's** walk to the park.
What is the best way to go?	**What's** the best way to go?
I would turn right here.	**I'd** turn right here.
That **is not** the way!	That **isn't** the way!

Underline the contraction in each sentence. Then write the two words that make the contraction.

1. Tito hasn't read the book. ______________
2. Nadia doesn't have a copy. ______________
3. Who'll lend Tito the book? ______________
4. We've seen plenty of copies in the library. ______________

Read each sentence. Replace the underlined words in the sentence with a contraction. Then write the sentence on the line.

5. The books <u>are not</u> on the shelf.

____

6. Lila <u>is not</u> here yet.

____

Name ______________________ Date ______________

Past Tense Irregular Verbs

Irregular past tense verbs do not end in **-ed**.

Present	**Past**	
get	got	I **got** a bike yesterday.
do	did	I **did** circles in the driveway.
ride	rode	Then I **rode** to school.
ring	rang	I **rang** the bell on my bike.

Choose the correct past tense verb from the box to complete each sentence. Write the verb on the line.

rode	do	ring	got
get	rang	did	ride

1. My alarm ______________ early this morning.

2. I ______________ my bike to school.

3. I ______________ well on the math test.

4. I ______________ a very high grade.

Rewrite the sentence using the past tense of the verb.

5. We ride on the train.

____

Name ______________________________ Date ____________________

Past Tense Irregular Verbs

Irregular past tense verbs do not end in **-ed**.

Present	**Past**	
send	sent	I **sent** a note last week.
say	said	I **said** hello.
leave	left	I **left** to visit Aunt Tisha.
wear	wore	I **wore** my new shoes.

Circle the form of the verb in ( ) that correctly completes the sentence. Write it on the line.

1. We (leave, left) ______________ the house last night.
2. We (said, say) ______________ good-bye to Mom.
3. Theo (wore, wear) ______________ a wrinkled shirt.
4. Dad (send, sent) ______________ him back.

Rewrite each sentence using the past tense of the verb.

5. I send a gift.

____

6. I say good-bye.

____

Name ______________________ Date ______________

Commas in Greetings and Closings

Letters and some journal entries begin with a greeting and end with a closing.

Greetings and closings are always followed by a comma.

Greetings	**Closings**
Hi, Lenny,	Your friend,
Dear Diary,	Joyfully,
Dear Mayor Brown,	Sincerely,

Circle whether each phrase is a greeting or a closing. Then rewrite it on the line, adding commas where needed.

1. Hello, Tom ______________ greeting closing

2. All my best ______________ greeting closing

3. Dear Diary ______________ greeting closing

4. Your pal ______________ greeting closing

5. With love ______________ greeting closing

Form a greeting by rewriting the words in the correct order and with the proper punctuation.

6. Jim Uncle Dear

____

Name ______________________ Date ______________

Commas in Greetings and Closings

Greetings and closings are always followed by a comma. Every word in a greeting begins with a capital letter. However, only the first word in a closing begins with a capital letter.

Dear Cole,
I had fun at your party.
Your pal,
Inez

Dear Diary,
We won the game!
Yours joyfully,
Brian

Read each greeting or closing. Then write it correctly on the line.

1. hi jane

____

2. your friend

____

3. dear aunt meg,

____

4. best wishes

____

5. dear cousin

____

6. until then

____

Form a closing by rewriting the words in the correct order and with the proper punctuation.

7. son your loving

____

Name ______________________ Date ______________

Capitalize Geographic Names

Geographic names are nouns that name places. Geographic names of specific places are proper nouns. Each word of a proper noun should begin with a capital letter.

Common Nouns	**Proper Nouns**
lake	Great Bear Lake
country	Canada
planet	Earth

Underline the geographic name in each sentence. Circle whether it is a common noun or a proper noun.

1. I live in New York. common noun proper noun
2. They lived on the prairie. common noun proper noun

Read each sentence. Then rewrite the sentence on the line with correct capitalization.

3. I went to california. ______________________
4. I saw the pacific ocean. ______________________
5. We stopped in san diego. ______________________
6. We visited mission beach. ______________________

Name ______________________________ Date ____________________

Capitalize Holidays

The names of specific holidays are proper nouns. Each word of a proper noun should begin with a capital letter.

We had a picnic on **Labor Day**.

I stayed up late on **New Year's Eve**.

Circle the holiday name in each sentence. Then write the name of the holiday correctly on the line.

1. School is closed on new year's day.

____

2. Is valentine's day your favorite holiday?

____

3. We planted a tree on arbor day.

____

4. What do you do on memorial day?

____

5. I watched fireworks on independence day.

____

6. My family gets together on thanksgiving.

____

Name ______________________________ Date ________________

Compound Sentences

In order to make a compound sentence, join two simple sentences together with a comma and a linking word such as **and** or **but**.

Simple sentences: I live in the desert. I like to hike.

Compound sentence: I live in the desert**, and** I like to hike.

Simple sentences: The days are hot. The nights are cool.

Compound sentence: The days are hot**, but** the nights are cool.

Read each compound sentence. Circle the linking word. Then write the two sentences that make up the compound sentence.

1. The beach is crowded, but we have fun.

______________________ ______________________

2. We swim in the water, and we play in the sand.

______________________ ______________________

3. I find shells, and Jess sees a crab.

______________________ ______________________

4. It is time to go, but we will be back.

______________________ ______________________

5. I want to go hiking, but I hurt my knee.

______________________ ______________________

Name ______________________________ Date ____________________

Compound Sentences

A compound sentence is formed when two simple sentences are put together. The simple sentences are combined using a comma and a linking word such as **and** or **but**.

Simple sentences: We went to the store. We bought fruit.

Compound sentence: We went to the store**, and** we bought fruit.

Simple sentences: I like apples. Wendy likes pears.

Compound sentence: I like apples**, but** Wendy likes pears.

Put the sentences together to make a compound sentence. Add a comma and the word *and*. Write the compound sentence on the line.

1. Mom gets a cart. Tina pushes.

____

2. They buy milk. They buy eggs.

____

Put the sentences together to make a compound sentence. Add a comma and the word *but*. Write the compound sentence on the line.

3. I am not tired. Lee is sleepy.

____

4. The salad is fresh. The bread is old.

____

Name ______________________________ Date ____________________

Dictionaries

Dictionaries give the spelling, pronunciation, part of speech, and meaning of words. All the words in a dictionary are listed in alphabetical order, from **a** to **z**. Words that begin with the same letter are put in alphabetical order according to the second letter.

ball (BAUL) *noun* a round object that can be thrown, hit, or kicked

blink (BLINK) *verb* to close and open your eyes fast

brag (BRAG) *verb* to talk too proudly about yourself

Read each group of words. Circle the word that would come first in a dictionary.

1. light loss late

2. envy empty ever

3. flag free foot

Alphabetize the words on the line in the order that they would appear in a dictionary.

4. track tire tug ______________________________

5. pony play pear ______________________________

6. shape snap sky ______________________________

7. gym gem glass ______________________________

Name ______________________ Date ______________

Dictionaries

Each print dictionary has two guide words at the top of every page. The first guide word is the first word on the page. The second guide word is the last word on the page. All the words that come between the two guide words make up the rest of the words on the page.

large • last

large (LARJ) *adjective* great in size

lark (LARK) *noun* 1. a small brown bird 2. a harmless prank

lasso (LA-soh) *noun* a rope with a large loop at the end

last (LAST) 1. *adjective* coming after all others
2. *verb* to go on for some time

For each set of guide words, circle the word you would find on the dictionary page.

1. hunk • hut	horse	hurt	head
2. anew • ankle	animal	America	asleep
3. vine • virus	vest	violin	voice
4. clown • coal	curl	crash	club
5. kink • knife	knee	koala	key
6. dizzy • dodge	dye	doctor	damp
7. may • measure	mouse	mild	maze

Name ______________________ Date ______________

Simple Sentences

A sentence is a group of words that tells a complete thought. A simple sentence has two parts. It has a pronoun or a noun that tells who or what does something, and a verb that tells what the person or thing does.

Simple Sentence	Who or What?	Does What?
Aunt Jen makes bread.	Aunt Jen	bread

Read each sentence. Draw a line under who or what does something. Circle what that person or thing does.

1. Rico and Carson visit the museum.

2. Rico looks at paintings.

3. Carson walks in the gardens.

Put the sentence parts together to make a complete simple sentence. Write the sentence on the line.

4. ate lunch. The students

____

5. Angie sipped juice.

____

6. drank milk Emma and Ned

____

Name ______________________________ Date ____________________

Compound Sentences

A compound sentence is made up of two simple sentences joined with a comma and a word such as **and** or **but**.

Ella dropped the vase. The vase broke.

Ella dropped the vase**, and** the vase broke.

Mom bought a new vase. It was too small.

Mom bought a new vase**, but** it was too small.

Combine the two simple sentences to make a compound sentence. Add a comma and the word *and* or *but*. Write the compound sentence on the line.

1. Luke reads. We listen.

____

2. The story is short. It is funny.

____

3. We laugh. We clap.

____

4. The day is cold. The sun is out.

____

5. We walk to the library. It is closed.

____

Name ______________________________ Date ____________________

Comparative Adjectives and Adverbs

Comparative adjectives and adverbs are used to compare things. Add **-er** or **-est** to most one-syllable adjectives and adverbs to create the comparative. Use **-er** to compare two things, and use **-est** to compare more than two things.

Adjectives	Adverbs
My turtle is **smaller** than my gerbil.	Buddy runs **faster** than Rusty.
My fish is the **smallest** of all.	The black dog runs the **fastest**.

Underline the comparative adjective or adverb in the sentence. Then circle whether it compares two or more than two.

1. Clare arrived sooner than Ben. two more than two

2. She worked harder than I did. two more than two

3. Clare is the nicest person I know. two more than two

Complete each sentence. On the line, write the correct comparative adjective or adverb in ( ).

4. The wind is (stronger, strongest) ______________ today than yesterday.

5. My kite flew (higher, highest) ______________ than Sam's kite.

Name ______________________________ Date ____________________

Comparative Adjectives and Adverbs

If an adjective or adverb has more than one syllable and does not end in **-y**, add **more** or **most** in front of the adjective or adverb to form the comparative. Use **more** to compare two things. Use **most** to compare more than two things.

Adjectives

Our porch is **more peaceful** than the living room.

My room is the **most peaceful** place of all.

Adverbs

Ava rides **more carefully** than Oliver.

Declan rides **most carefully** of all.

Underline the words that compare things in each sentence. Then circle whether the words compare two or more than two.

1. Rita dances more gracefully than I do.

two more than two

2. Bea is the most beautiful dancer in the class.

two more than two

3. Mrs. Kent is the most skillful dance teacher of all.

two more than two

4. Of all our neighbors, Mr. Bruno holds cookouts most often.

two more than two

Name ______________________________ Date ________________

Combine Sentences

Two short sentences that are related can be combined into one sentence. This will help eliminate repetition and make your writing sound better.

Henry forgot his homework. Henry forgot his lunch.
Henry forgot his homework and his lunch.

Rewrite each sentence pair combining the two sentences into one sentence.

1. My sister plays soccer. My brother plays soccer.

____

2. The puppy was hungry. The puppy was thirsty.

____

3. Jorge wore a red hat. Jorge wore a red sweater.

____

4. My dad has a new rake. My dad has a new shovel.

____

5. Zoe opened the door. Zoe opened the window.

____

Name ______________________ Date ______________

Adjectives

Adjectives describe or tell more about nouns or pronouns. Adjectives can give more information about size, color, number, and kind.

The **brown** dog jumped over the fence.
Alex was carrying **huge** packages.

Underline the adjective in each sentence and circle the noun it describes.

1. Alisa wore blue shoes to school today.
2. Elena makes delicious meals.
3. Everyone was excited about meeting new friends.
4. Eliot planted yellow flowers.
5. Alisa draws beautiful pictures.
6. Andrew collects old coins.
7. My dog doesn't like loud storms.
8. Jonas drew colorful drawings.
9. I love rainy days.
10. Liam brought red apples.

Name ______________________ Date ______________

Contractions

A contraction is a shortened form of a word or words. An apostrophe takes the place of the dropped letters in a contraction.

I **was not** able to go.
I **wasn't** able to go.

Underline the contraction in each sentence. Then write the word or words that make the contraction.

1. I've never been to the circus. ______________

2. The artist hasn't sold any of his paintings. ______________

3. Jenna can't find her book. ______________

4. Who'll be coming to the party? ______________

5. Don't forget to bring your lunch. ______________

Rewrite each sentence replacing the underlined words with a contraction.

6. The catcher did not come to the baseball game.

____

7. Samantha could not bring her brother to school.

____

Name ______________________ Date ______________

Commas

Commas are used to set off introductory clauses or phrases in a sentence.

Later in the day, we will visit the museum.

Put a comma after the introductory phrase or clause in each sentence below.

1. Before Juno became goalie the team had lost all of its games.
2. When the rain started we ran off the field.
3. While we were hiking I saw two chipmunks.
4. After putting on her helmet Nina rode off on her bike.
5. To prepare for the picnic we bought some watermelon.

Rewrite each sentence using commas correctly.

6. Before Sean left the party he said good-bye to everyone.

____

7. While we are waiting let's eat our snacks.

____

Name ______________________________ Date ____________________

Irregular Plural Nouns

A plural noun names more than one person, place, or thing. Regular plural nouns end in **-s.** Irregular plural nouns do not have any spelling rules or patterns.

One	More Than One	One	More Than One
person	people	mouse	mice
child	children	cactus	cacti
goose	geese	shelf	shelves

Choose the plural noun from the box that best completes each sentence. Write it on the line.

geese	shelf	children	cactus
cacti	child	goose	shelves

1. There are twenty happy ______________ in our classroom.

2. All the ______________ are filled with books.

3. We read a book about a bunch of honking ______________.

4. We have two ______________ growing on the windowsill.

Rewrite each sentence using an irregular plural noun.

5. I see three gray mouse.

____

6. Many person came to my party.

____

Name ______________________________ Date ________________

Irregular Plural Nouns

A plural noun names more than one person, place, or thing. Irregular plural nouns have no spelling rules.

One	More Than One	One	More Than One
foot	feet	calf	calves
wolf	wolves	tooth	teeth
life	lives	woman	women

Choose the plural noun from the box that best completes each sentence. Write it on the line.

life	teeth	wolf	calf
tooth	calves	lives	wolves

1. There are two new ______________ on the farm.

2. Dogs are tame, but ______________ are wild.

3. The ______________ of a shark are very sharp.

4. Cats really do not have nine ______________.

Rewrite each sentence using an irregular plural noun.

5. Three woman own the farm.

____

6. The dog is three foot long.

____

Name ______________________________ Date ____________________

Possessives

A possessive shows ownership. Add an apostrophe and **s** to the end of a singular noun to form a possessive. For a plural noun that ends in **s**, add an apostrophe to the end of the noun to form a possessive.

Singular (One)	Plural (More Than One)
Mom's ring	**girls'** shirts
store's parking lot	**customers'** carts
pond's water	**lakes'** shores

Circle the correct possessive. Write it on the line.

1. The ____________ hallway is noisy. school's schools'

2. All the ____________ faces are friendly. teacher's teachers'

3. Our ______________ computer is new. classroom's classrooms'

4. The ______________ desks are comfortable. student's students'

Rewrite each sentence using a possessive. Replace the underlined words.

5. I like <u>the hat that belongs to Emily</u>.

____

6. <u>The shoes of the boys</u> are muddy.

____

Name ______________________________ Date ____________________

Possessives

A possessive shows ownership. Add an apostrophe and **s** to the end of a singular noun to form a possessive. For a plural noun that ends in **s**, add an apostrophe to the end of the noun to form a possessive.

Singular (One)	**Plural (More Than One)**
girl's bike	**girls'** bikes
town's park	**towns'** parks

Rewrite each sentence using a possessive. Replace the underlined words.

1. <u>The garden of my mother</u> is big.

____

2. <u>The colors of the flowers</u> are pretty.

____

3. <u>The thorns on the roses</u> are sharp.

____

4. <u>The dog that belongs to Noah</u> digs holes in the garden.

____

5. <u>The bone of the dog</u> is buried in the dirt.

____

6. <u>The acorns of squirrels</u> are buried there, too.

____

Name ______________________________ Date ____________________

Adjectives

Adjectives tell about a person, place, or thing. Adjectives describe the color, number, or size of an object.

Ben has a **big** bag.
Kim has a **blue** lunch box.
I have **three** apples.

Read each sentence. Circle the noun and underline the adjective.

1. I dislike the hot weather.

2. I bought two shirts.

3. I saw a large bird.

Underline the adjective in each sentence. Then circle whether the adjective describes color, number, or size.

4. There are six grapes in the bowl. Color Number Size

5. The red bowl is on the counter. Color Number Size

6. I see a large plate in the cabinet. Color Number Size

Name ______________________________ Date ____________________

Adverbs

Adverbs describe verbs. They give details about how, when, or where an action happens.

We spoke **clearly**. We recited the poem **before**.
I left my book **somewhere**. James **quickly** found it.

Read each sentence. Circle the verb and underline the adverb.

1. I happily agreed to be in the play.

2. All the actors practiced daily.

3. We presented the play outdoors.

4. My friends performed beautifully.

5. We threw a party afterward.

Underline the adverb in each sentence. Then circle whether the adverb tells who, when, or where.

6. Weeds grow everywhere. How When Where

7. Sophia carefully pulls them. How When Where

8. Soon vegetable plants sprout. How When Where

Name ______________________ Date ______________

Adverbs and Adjectives

Adverbs describe verbs. Adjectives describe nouns.
Add **-ly** to the end of most adjectives to turn them into adverbs.

Adjective: My new shoes are **perfect**!

Adverb: My new shoes fit **perfectly**!

Complete each sentence by writing the adjective or the adverb on the line.

1. The ______________ flight took only an hour.
shortly short

2. Mia ____________ preordered the book.
excitedly exciting

3. I rode my bike very ______________.
quickly quick

4. They will ______________ be able to fix my broken bike.
hopefully hopeful

5. We went to the museum to see ______________ art.
beautifully beautiful

6. You have to talk ______________ in the library.
quietly quiet

Name ______________________________ Date ________________

Adverbs and Adjectives

Adverbs describe verbs, while adjectives describe nouns. Add **-ly** to the end of most adjectives to turn them into adverbs.

Adjective: The **brave** firefighters finished putting out the fire.

Adverb: The firefighters **bravely** put out the fire.

Choose the correct word from the box to complete each sentence. Write the adjective or adverb on the line.

strange	strangely	happy	loudly
happily	loud	sweet	sweetly

1. Caleb picked up the ______________ object to figure out what it was.
2. Bananas are a very ______________ fruit.
3. I spoke ______________ to be heard over the music.
4. I ran around ______________ once we got to the beach.
5. My shirt fit ______________ after I grew taller.
6. The roar of the airplane was so ______________!
7. My grandmother very ______________ made me a new sweater.

Name ______________________________ Date ____________________

Past Tense Irregular Verbs

Most past tense verbs end in **-ed**. Some verbs, however, do not follow this spelling pattern in their past tense form. These are called irregular verbs.

Present Tense	**Irregular Past Tense**
give	gave
run	ran
see	saw
write	wrote

Choose the correct past tense verb from the box to complete each sentence. Write the verb on the line.

run	give	ran	wrote
write	saw	gave	see

1. We ______________ a baseball game on Saturday.

2. Kim ______________ to first base.

3. The coach ______________ Kim a high-five.

4. I ______________ a journal entry about the game.

Rewrite each sentence using the past tense of the verb.

5. I see a parade. ____________________

6. I give her an apple. ____________________

Name ______________________________ Date ____________________

Past Tense Irregular Verbs

Regular past tense verbs end in **-ed**. Irregular past tense verbs have no spelling rules.

Present Tense	Irregular Past Tense
feel	felt
go	went
make	made
eat	ate

Write the correct form of the verb in ( ) to complete each sentence.

1. The boys (felt, feel) ______________ hungry.

2. They (make, made) ______________ a snack.

3. They (eat, ate) ______________ apples and cheese.

4. Then they (went, go) ______________ to the park.

Rewrite each sentence using the past tense of the verb.

5. I go to class. ______________________________

6. I make a bookmark. ______________________________

Name ______________________________ Date ____________________

Simple Sentences

A simple sentence tells a complete thought. It tells who or what does something.

Simple Sentence	**Who or What?**	**Does What?**
Dan throws a ball.	Dan	throws a ball
Will Sparky fetch the ball?	Sparky	fetch the ball
Get the ball, Sparky!	Sparky	get the ball

Put the words together to form a complete simple sentence. Write the simple sentence on the line.

1. The girls walk to school.

____

2. rides the bus. Ben

____

3. stop here? Will the bus

____

4. Ben runs fast!

____

5. bus driver! Stop,

____

Name ______________________________ Date ____________________

Compound Sentences

A compound sentence is made up of two simple sentences. The sentences are joined with a comma and a linking word such as **and** or **but**.

Simple Sentences: I went to the library. I found a good book.

Compound Sentence: I went to the library**, and** I found a good book.

Combine the simple sentences to make a compound sentence. Add a comma and the word *and.* Write the compound sentence on the line.

1. We went to the zoo. We had fun.

____

2. I rode a pony. Dad rode a camel.

____

Combine the simple sentences to make a compound sentence. Add a comma and the word *but.* Write the compound sentence on the line.

3. Dad likes lions. I like bears.

____

4. We saw zebras. We did not see giraffes.

____

Name ______________________ Date ______________

Proper Nouns

Proper nouns name specific people, places, or things. Each word of a proper noun should begin with a capital letter.

Common Noun	**Proper Noun**
boy	Roger
park	Yellowstone
state	Wyoming
country	United States

Underline the proper noun in each sentence.

1. I live in Buffalo.

2. My best friend is Anya.

3. We went to Niagara Falls together.

Choose a proper noun from the box to complete each sentence. Write it on the line.

Arizona	Grand Canyon	Pam

4. I visited my friend ______________________.

5. She lives in ______________________.

6. The ______________________ is huge!

Name ______________________________ Date ____________________

Proper Nouns

Proper nouns name specific people, places, or things. Each word of a proper noun should begin with a capital letter.

People	**Places**	**Things**
Rahul	California	Pacific Ocean
Thomas	New York	Central Park
Mia	Washington, D.C.	White House

Underline the proper noun in each sentence. Then write the proper noun correctly on the line.

1. I live in the city of chicago. ____________________

2. I live with aunt kim. ____________________

3. We shop on michigan avenue. ____________________

4. We walk along lakefront road. ____________________

Read each sentence. Then write it correctly on the line.

5. The metropolitan museum is amazing!

____

6. I can't wait to visit new york city again!

____

Name ______________________________ Date ________________

Adjectives

Adjectives describe or tell more about nouns or pronouns.

Stones made it difficult to hike.

Slippery stones made it difficult to hike.

Underline the adjective in each sentence. Circle the word it describes.

1. Adam has three brothers.

2. Everyone enjoyed the beautiful weather.

3. We woke up to blue skies.

4. A giant boulder blocked our path.

Choose the adjective from the box that best completes each sentence. Write it on the line.

red	deep	tiny	two

5. The ________________ kitten started to purr.

6. My brother read ________________ books this week.

7. Ted rides a ________________ bike to school.

8. We had to walk in ________________ snow to get to school.

Name ______________________________ Date ________________

Formal and Informal Language

Formal language consists of complete sentences and standard grammar. You should use formal language when writing an academic essay. Informal language consists of incomplete sentences and slang. Use informal language in friendly pieces of writing such as an e-mail or a letter to friends or family members.

Formal	**Informal**
Good night, Miss Lopez.	Bye Ashley. I'm out!
In my opinion, this is correct.	I think it's OK, you know?

For each example, circle whether the language is formal or informal.

1. Good morning, Mr. Mayor. May we ask you about the weather emergency?

Formal Informal

2. Hey! Did you see those cool thunderclouds? They were awesome!

Formal Informal

3. Weather experts reported seeing two funnel clouds yesterday.

Formal Informal

4. Was I scared? Sure! It was so windy. I thought for sure the house would fall down!

Formal Informal

Name ______________________ Date ______________

Capitalize Proper Nouns

Each word of a proper noun should begin with a capital letter. The titles and names of people, the days of the week, and the months of the year are all examples of proper nouns.

Title and Name	**Day**	**Month**
Ms. Olivia Trent	Sunday	January

Circle the proper noun in each sentence. Then write it correctly on the line.

1. Our principal's name is mrs. lara garcia. ______________

2. Have you met officer bill brown? ______________

3. I have an appointment with my dentist, dr. paul costa.

____

Circle whether each word names a day or a month. Then write the proper noun correctly on the line.

4. tuesday ______________ Day Month

5. june ______________ Day Month

6. april ______________ Day Month

Name ______________________ Date ______________

Capitalize Geographic Names and Holidays

The names of specific geographic places or sites around the world are proper nouns. The names of specific holidays are also proper nouns. Each word of a proper noun should begin with a capital letter.

Geographic Names	**Holidays**
Rocky Mountains	Independence Day
Mississippi River	Labor Day

Underline the geographic name in each sentence. Then write the sentence correctly on the line.

1. I live on elm street. ______________________

2. Emily lives near lake michigan. ______________________

3. We took a trip to florida. ______________________

Underline the holiday in each sentence. Then write the sentence correctly on the line.

4. We watched a parade on thanksgiving.

____

5. Is our school open on presidents' day?

____

6. We plant trees on arbor day.

____

Name ______________________________ Date ____________________

Simple and Compound Sentences

A sentence is a group of words that tells a complete thought. To form a compound sentence, join two or more simple sentences with a comma and a linking word such as **and**, **but**, or **or**.

Simple Sentences	**Compound Sentence**
I like music. I like to read.	I like music**, and** I like to read.

Underline both simple sentences that form the compound sentence. Circle the word that joins the sentences.

1. Ryan lost his library book, and Jose found it.

2. Kayla likes nonfiction, but Nathan likes folktales.

3. I will meet you at the library, or I will see you later.

Combine the two simple sentences to make a compound sentence. Add a comma and a linking word. Write the compound sentence on the line.

4. Julie shouted hello. I answered.

____

5. We got on our bikes. We rode to the store.

____

6. She got some juice. I bought crackers.

____

Name ______________________________ Date ____________________

Simple and Compound Sentences

A compound sentence is made of two or more simple sentences. The sentences are joined by a comma and a linking word such as **and**, **but**, or **or**.

Simple Sentences	**Compound Sentence**
It is cool now. It will be warm later.	It is cool now**, but** it will be warm later.

Combine the two simple sentences to make a compound sentence. Add a comma and a linking word. Write the compound sentence on the line.

1. It rained last night. The sky is clear tonight.

____

2. We see many stars. The moon is shining brightly.

____

3. We can gaze at the stars. We can watch TV.

____

4. You can wear a sweater. You can put on a coat.

____

5. Hank might stay up. He might go to bed.

____

Name ______________________________ Date ____________________

Contractions

A contraction is a shortened form of a word or words. An apostrophe replaces the dropped letter or letters in a contraction.

I will go to the party. **I'll** go to the party.

Underline each contraction. On the line, write the word or words that form it.

1. Let's meet before the game. ______________
2. The rain can't get in the way of our plans! ______________
3. I guess we'll see my sister out on the field. ______________
4. I don't like the rain. ______________
5. It isn't fair that we have to stay inside! ______________
6. Zeke didn't get my e-mail, so I will resend it. ______________
7. David is not able to exercise today, so he'll run tomorrow.

   ____
8. I think they're on their way! ______________

Name ______________________ Date ______________

Possessives

A possessive shows to what or to whom something belongs. Add an apostrophe and an **s** to a singular noun to form a singular possessive. Add an apostrophe to a plural noun that ends in **s** to form a plural possessive.

Singular Possessive	Plural Possessive
Ella's quilt is handmade.	The **babies'** blankets are new.
The **farm's** strawberries are ripe.	The **pickers'** baskets are full.

Rewrite each sentence, replacing the underlined words with a possessive phrase.

1. The <u>gates of the zoo</u> are open.

____

2. I want to see the <u>habitat of the penguins.</u>

____

3. The <u>paw of the polar bear</u> is huge!

____

4. Did you see the <u>cubs of the lions</u>?

____

5. The <u>tail of the peacock</u> is beautiful.

____

6. When is the <u>feeding time of the tigers</u>?

____

Name ______________________________ Date ____________________

Adjectives

Adjectives describe nouns. Adjectives can give information about color, number, size, and kind. In the phrase **the blue rug**, the adjective **blue** tells the color of the noun **rug**.

Circle the adjective in each sentence. Underline the noun or nouns it describes.

1. Olivia looked into her messy closet.
2. She was looking for her favorite shirt and pants.
3. Anya enjoys planting beautiful flowers in the garden.
4. Ann dislikes buying new clothes.
5. Bryn thinks that the field is huge.
6. That annoying phone keeps ringing!
7. Anna's youngest sister misbehaves.
8. Max's older brother is nice.
9. The city has a lot of tall buildings.
10. The theater has a big stage.

Name ______________________ Date ______________

Capitalize Geographic Names

Geographic names of specific places are proper nouns. Each word in a geographic name should begin with a capital letter.

Geographic Names

Brooklyn Bridge

North Carolina

San Francisco

Circle the geographic name in each sentence. Then write it correctly on the line.

1. I am going on a trip to charlottesville. ______________

2. It is a city in the state of virginia. ______________

3. I went hiking in the rocky mountain national park.

____

4. The park is in colorado. ______________

5. There are many musicals to see in new york city.

____

6. The capital city is albany. ______________

7. Someday, I want to visit italy. ______________

Name ______________________________ Date ____________________

Contractions

A contraction is a shortened form of a word or words. An apostrophe replaces the dropped letter or letters in a contraction.

Contraction	Words That Make Up the Contraction
doesn't	does not
he's	he is
we're	we are
it'll	it will

Underline each contraction. On the line, write the two words that form it.

1. The team didn't score many points. __________

2. We weren't impressed by their performance. __________

3. Who's going to the game next week? __________

4. I've already bought my tickets. __________

Rewrite each sentence, replacing the underlined words in the sentence with a contraction.

5. <u>I will</u> see you at the game! ____________________________

6. <u>We are</u> getting there early. ____________________________

Name ______________________________ Date ____________________

Contractions and Possessives

An apostrophe replaces the dropped letter or letters in a contraction. An apostrophe is also used to form a possessive noun to show to what or to whom something belongs.

Contraction	Possessive
Emma is my best friend.	**The sweater that belongs to Emma** is red.
Emma's my best friend.	**Emma's sweater** is red.

For each sentence, circle whether the underlined word is a contraction or a possessive.

1. Is Kyra's birthday next week? Contraction Possessive
2. Let's have a party! Contraction Possessive
3. She'll be surprised. Contraction Possessive
4. I have her friends' addresses. Contraction Possessive

Rewrite each sentence, replacing the underlined words with a contraction or a possessive.

5. The party is at the house belonging to Mark.

   ____

6. Please do not be late. ____________________

Name ______________________________ Date ____________________

Proper Nouns

Proper nouns name specific people, places, and things. Each word in a proper noun is capitalized.

People	Places	Things
Lila	Kansas City	Brooklyn Bridge
Ed Hall	New Mexico	Memorial Day
Mrs. Chopra	Canada	Washington Monument

Underline the proper noun in each sentence. Then write the proper noun correctly on the line.

1. My family went boating on lake mead. ____________________

2. We saw hoover dam the next day. ____________________

3. Then we went hiking in black canyon. ____________________

4. Our guide was named dan adams. ____________________

Read each sentence. Then rewrite it correctly on the line.

5. I will visit aunt sue in florida.

____

6. She lives on orange tree drive.

____

Name ______________________ Date ______________

Comparative Adjectives and Adverbs

Add **-er** to most one-syllable adjectives and adverbs to compare two things. Add **-est** to most one-syllable adjectives and adverbs to compare more than two things. If an adjective or adverb has more than one syllable and does not end in **-y**, use **more** to compare two things and **most** to compare more than two things.

Compare Two	Compare More Than Two
We took the **shorter** of the two trails.	The east trail is the **longest** of all.
I walked **slower** than Liam.	Karen walked the **fastest**.
This trail is **more rugged** than the last.	Which trail is the **most scenic**?

Underline the comparative adjective or adverb. Then circle whether it compares two or more than two.

1. Pete worked harder than I did.

two more than two

2. His origami creations were nicer than mine.

two more than two

3. The most talented artist won the competition.

two more than two

4. Diving seems more difficult than swimming.

two more than two

Name ______________________ Date ______________

Contractions and Possessives

A contraction is a shortened form of a word or words. When writing a contraction, use an apostrophe to replace the dropped letters. Possessives show ownership. Use an apostrophe in a possessive to show who or what has something or owns it.

Contraction	Possessive
Let us go to the store.	**The friend of Jason** wants a new belt.
Let's go to the store.	**Jason's friend** wants a new belt.

Rewrite each sentence on the line, replacing the underlined words with a contraction.

1. <u>I am</u> looking for a white shirt. ______________________

2. <u>He is</u> going to buy jeans. ______________________

3. <u>Where is</u> the closest mall? ______________________

Rewrite each sentence on the line, replacing the underlined words with a possessive phrase.

4. <u>The shoe size of Meg</u> is smaller than mine.

____

5. <u>The manager of the store</u> was polite.

____

Name ________________________________ Date ____________________

Complete Sentences

A sentence is a group of words that tells a complete thought. A complete simple sentence has two parts: a subject and a verb. A subject tells who or what did something. A verb tells what the person or thing did.

Complete Sentence	Who or What?	Did What?
My family went on a picnic.	My family	went on a picnic
My cousins and I played catch.	My cousins and I	played catch

Read each sentence. Underline who or what does something. Circle what that person or thing does.

1. Tall trees shaded our picnic table.

2. Belinda and I unpacked the lunch.

3. Aunt Rita's salad had a mixture of fruit.

Put the words together to form a complete sentence. Write the sentence on the line.

4. flew a kite My brother

____

5. Uncle Rick played his guitar

____

Name ______________________________ Date ________________

Dictionaries

You can use a dictionary to check the spelling, pronunciation, and meaning of words. Words in dictionaries are organized in alphabetical order. Print dictionaries have two guide words at the top of each page. The first guide word is the first word on the page. The second guide word is the last word on the page.

pester • pheasant

pester (PES-ter) *verb* to annoy someone

pet (PET) *noun* a tame animal; *verb* to stroke

pheasant (FEH-zunt) *noun* a large bird with a long tail

Write the words in alphabetical order or how they would appear in a dictionary. Alphabetize to the second letter.

1. rye ruin roll ______________________

2. meter magma mountain ______________________

3. sculpture stretch shadow ______________________

For each set of guide words, circle the word you would find on the dictionary page.

4. bowl • brake blue brain butterfly

5. live • loan lizard lunch leave

6. any • apiece arrow actor apart

Name ______________________________ Date ____________________

Commas

Commas are punctuation marks that signal a pause or connect ideas. Use a comma after a greeting and after a closing in a letter or journal entry. Use a comma before a conjunction when joining two simple sentences to form a compound sentence.

Dear Miguel**,**

I went on vacation**, and** I had a great time. I rafted each day**, or** I hiked.

The mountain peaks were jagged**, but** they were beautiful.

Your friend**,**

Noah

Read each greeting or closing below. Then rewrite it with the correct punctuation.

1. Hi Jack ________________

2. Your pal ________________

3. Dear Ethan ________________

4. Best wishes ________________

Combine the two simple sentences to make a compound sentence. Use a comma and the word in ( ). Write the compound sentence on the line.

5. The city was fun. It was crowded. (but)

____

6. We rode on buses. We took taxis. (and)

____

Spelling
&
Vocabulary

Name ______________________ Date ______________

Short Vowels

wet	jump	this	box	him
stand	chest	flag	run	shop

Write the spelling word for each clue.

1. It starts like **red** and ends like **fun**. ______________
2. It starts like **jet** and ends like **bump**. ______________
3. It starts like **ham** and ends like **dim**. ______________
4. It starts like **bed** and ends like **fox**. ______________
5. It starts like **win** and ends like **pet**. ______________
6. It starts like **shed** and ends like **top**. ______________
7. It starts like **chin** and ends like **best**. ______________

Write a spelling word to complete each sentence.

8. I like ______________ book.
9. I ______________ and read aloud in class.
10. We raised the ______________ to the top of the pole.

Name ______________________ Date ______________

Short Vowels

wet	jump	this	box	him
stand	chest	flag	run	shop

Write the correct spelling words.

Spelling words with short vowel *a*

1. ______________ **2.** ______________

Spelling words with short vowel *e*

3. ______________ **4.** ______________

Spelling words with short vowel *i*

5. ______________ **6.** ______________

Spelling words with short vowel *o*

7. ______________ **8.** ______________

Spelling words with short vowel *u*

9. ______________ **10.** ______________

Name ______________________________ Date ____________________

Open and Closed Syllables

she	napkin	we	silent	go
hi	open	dentist	no	problem

Write the spelling word for each clue.

1. You wipe your mouth on this. ________________

2. This person fixes teeth. ________________

3. You say this when you don't agree. ________________

4. This describes people in a library. ________________

5. You do this to a box or an envelope. ________________

6. You can say this instead of hello. ________________

7. This is something to figure out. ________________

8. This is a pronoun for a girl. ________________

9. This is a pronoun used for more than one person. ________

10. This is an action verb. ________________

Name ______________________________ Date ____________________

Open and Closed Syllables

she	napkin	we	silent	go
hi	open	dentist	no	problem

Write the correct spelling words.

Spelling words with one open syllable

1. ____________ **2.** ____________

3. ____________ **4.** ____________

5. ____________

Spelling words with one open and one closed syllable

6. ____________ **7.** ____________

Spelling words with two closed syllables

8. ____________ **9.** ____________

10. ____________

Write the spelling word that is the opposite of the bold word.

11. come ____________ **12. noisy** ____________

Name ______________________________ Date ____________________

Long a: ai, ea, ay

rain	great	play	mail	stay
day	chain	break	say	paint

Circle the spelling word that completes the sentence. Then write it on the line.

1. I ______________ with my dog.

rain break play

2. Dad and Ben ______________ the fence.

stay paint mail

3. We eat a ______________ lunch.

great chain paint

4. It has been a good ______________!

rain day say

Fill in the boxes for the spelling word *stay*.

word meaning	**sentence**
stay	
synonym	**antonym**

Name ______________________ Date ______________

Long a: ai, ea, ay

rain	great	play	mail	stay
day	chain	break	say	paint

Write the correct spelling words.

Spelling words with long *a* spelled *ai*

1. ______________ **2.** ______________

3. ______________ **4.** ______________

Spelling words with long *a* spelled *ay*

5. ______________ **6.** ______________

7. ______________ **8.** ______________

Spelling words with long *a* spelled *ea*

9. ______________ **10.** ______________

In each row, circle the two spelling words that rhyme.

11. rain mail chain

12. great play stay

Name ______________________ Date ______________

Long o: oa, o, ow

roast	both	grow	cold	throw
going	float	loaf	bowl	soap

Write the spelling words for each clue.

1. toss something into the air ______________

2. a curved dish ______________

3. low temperature; very chilly ______________

4. bread baked in one piece ______________

5. cook something in an oven ______________

6. two people or things together ______________

Circle the two spelling words that rhyme.

7. going throw soap grow

 Grammar, Spelling & Vocabulary Activity Book •

Name ______________________________ Date ________________

Long o: oa, o, ow

roast	both	grow	cold	throw
going	float	loaf	bowl	soap

Write the spelling words that match each long *o* spelling.

Spelling words with long *o* spelled *o*

1. ________________ **2.** ________________

3. ________________

Spelling words with long *o* spelled *oa*

4. ________________ **5.** ________________

6. ________________ **7.** ________________

Spelling words with long *o* spelled *ow*

8. ________________ **9.** ________________

10. ________________

Name ______________________ Date ______________

Long e: ee, ea, y, ey, ie

happy	queen	clean	key	read
tree	funny	piece	leaf	need

Write the spelling word for each clue.

1. She is the ruler of a country. ______________
2. This is part of a plant. ______________
3. This large plant has a trunk. ______________
4. A joke should be this. ______________
5. You smile when you feel this way. ______________
6. This is used to open a lock. ______________
7. You do this to a book. ______________
8. This means "must have." ______________
9. This is one part of something. ______________
10. You do this when you sweep or mop. ______________

Name ______________________ Date ______________

Long e: ee, ea, y, ey, ie

happy	queen	clean	key	read
tree	funny	piece	leaf	need

Write the spelling words that match each long *e* spelling.

Spelling words with long *e* spelled *ea*

1. ____________ **2.** ____________

3. ____________

Spelling words with long *e* spelled *ee*

4. ____________ **5.** ____________

6. ____________

Spelling word with long *e* spelled *ey*

7. ____________

Spelling word with long *e* spelled *ie*

8. ____________

Spelling words with long *e* spelled *y*

9. ____________ **10.** ____________

Name ______________________ Date ______________

Long i: ie, i, y, igh

high	child	dry	night	tried
sky	bright	cried	kind	light

Write a spelling word to complete each sentence.

1. Jeff helps me ____________ the dishes.

2. The baby ____________ when she was hungry.

3. Please turn on the ____________ in the hall.

4. There are many clouds in the ____________.

5. A ____________ played with the toy.

6. The nest is ____________ in the tree.

7. Dad ____________ to fix the car.

8. It is ____________ of you to help me.

Read the spelling word below. Write two spelling words that rhyme with it.

9. light ____________ ____________

Name ______________________ Date ______________

Long i: ie, i, y, igh

high	child	dry	night	tried
sky	bright	cried	kind	light

Write the spelling words that match each long *i* spelling.

Spelling words with long *i* spelled *i*

1. ________________ **2.** ________________

Spelling words with long *i* spelled *ie*

3. ________________ **4.** ________________

Spelling words with long *i* spelled *igh*

5. ________________ **6.** ________________

7. ________________ **8.** ________________

Spelling words with long *i* spelled *y*

9. ________________ **10.** ________________

Write the spelling word that is the opposite of each word below.

11. wet ________________ **12.** dark ________________

Name ______________________ Date ______________

Long u: ew, ue, u, u_e

few	cube	January	rescue	cute
menu	huge	fuel	music	use

Write the spelling word for each clue.

1. You read it in a restaurant. ______________

2. It is the opposite of little. ______________

3. It is the name of a month. ______________

4. A bus needs it to run. ______________

5. It is the opposite of many. ______________

6. It is a shape. ______________

7. You hear it when a band plays. ______________

Write the spelling word that completes each sentence.

8. We will ______________ a puppy from the shelter.

9. The tiny puppy is ______________.

10. I ______________ a brush on its fur.

Name ______________________ Date ______________

Long u : ew, ue, u, u_e

few	cube	January	rescue	cute
menu	huge	fuel	music	use

Write the spelling words for the given long *u* spelling.

Spelling words with long *u* spelled *u_e*

1. ______________ **2.** ______________

3. ______________ **4.** ______________

Spelling word with long *u* spelled *ew*

5. ______________

Spelling words with long *u* spelled *ue*

6. ______________ **7.** ______________

Spelling words with long *u* spelled *u*

8. ______________ **9.** ______________

10. ______________

Name ______________________________ Date ____________________

r-Controlled Vowel ar

garden	march	car	yard	large
star	hard	smart	shark	farm

Circle the spelling word that completes each sentence. Then write it on the line.

1. A ______________ has many teeth.

star garden shark

2. Cows live on a ______________.

yard farm car

3. An elephant is a ______________ animal.

large garden march

4. A clam has a ______________ shell.

smart hard star

5. Dolphins are very ______________.

hard march smart

6. Sometimes rabbits eat plants in a ______________.

garden car shark

Name ______________________ Date ______________

r-Controlled Vowel ar

garden	march	car	yard	large
star	hard	smart	shark	farm

Write the correct spelling words.

Spelling words that end with *ar*

1. ______________ **2.** ______________

4-letter spelling words with *ar*

3. ______________ **4.** ______________

5. ______________

5-letter spelling words with *ar*

6. ______________ **7.** ______________

8. ______________ **9.** ______________

2-syllable spelling word with *ar*

10. ______________

Name ______________________________ Date ____________________

r-Controlled Vowels er, ir, ur

her	bird	never	burn	winter
third	hurt	shirt	girl	nurse

Write the spelling word that matches each definition.

1. a piece of clothing ______________

2. a cold season of the year ______________

3. person who cares for sick people ______________

4. not at any time ______________

5. coming after two other things ______________

6. to feel pain ______________

Fill in the boxes for the spelling word *bird*.

word meaning	sentence
examples	**things it does**

bird

 G2 U3 W3 BLM1

Name ______________________________ Date ____________________

r-Controlled Vowels er, ir, ur

her	bird	never	burn	winter
third	hurt	shirt	girl	nurse

Write the spelling words for the given r-controlled vowel spelling pattern.

Spelling words with *er*

1. ____________________ **2.** ____________________

3. ____________________

Spelling words with *ir*

4. ____________________ **5.** ____________________

6. ____________________ **7.** ____________________

Spelling words with *ur*

8. ____________________ **9.** ____________________

10. ____________________

Circle the two spelling words that rhyme.

11. bird hurt third burn

Name ______________________________ Date ________________

r-Controlled Vowels or, oar, ore

store	oars	fork	before	wore
more	horn	roar	sports	born

Write the spelling word that completes each sentence.

1. Nick was ______________ in June.

2. He likes to watch ______________.

3. Nick got a team shirt at the ______________.

4. He ______________ the shirt at the game.

5. Listen to the crowd ______________!

6. Jill's dad has ______________ than one boat.

7. One of the boats has a loud ______________.

8. We need ______________ to row this boat.

9. Have you rowed a boat ______________?

10. Jill needs a ______________ to eat her lunch.

Name ____________________ Date ____________

r-Controlled Vowels or, oar, ore

store	oars	fork	before	wore
more	horn	roar	sports	born

Write the spelling words that match the given spelling.

r-controlled vowel spelled *ore*

1. ____________ **2.** ____________

3. ____________ **4.** ____________

r-controlled vowel spelled *or*

5. ____________ **6.** ____________

7. ____________ **8.** ____________

r-controlled vowel spelled *oar*

9. ____________ **10.** ____________

Circle the two spelling words that rhyme.

11. oars wore sports store

12. horn roar fork born

Name ______________________________ Date ____________________

r-Controlled Vowels ear, eer, ere

hear	steer	year	near	deer
clear	ears	cheer	fear	here

Write the spelling word for each clue.

1. These animals live in the woods. ______________
2. A driver does this with a wheel of a car. ______________
3. It describes a sky without clouds. ______________
4. You hear and listen with these. ______________
5. It is made up of twelve months. ______________
6. You do it with one of your five senses. ______________
7. You might hear the crowd at a game do this. ________
8. It means "close to." ______________
9. It is what you feel when you are afraid. ______________
10. It means "at this place." ______________

Name ______________________________ Date ____________________

r-Controlled Vowels ear, eer, ere

hear	steer	year	near	deer
clear	ears	cheer	fear	here

Write the spelling words that match the given spelling patterns.

r-controlled vowel spelled *ear*

1. ______________________ **2.** ______________________

3. ______________________ **4.** ______________________

5. ______________________ **6.** ______________________

r-controlled vowel spelled *eer*

7. ______________________ **8.** ______________________

9. ______________________

r-controlled vowel spelled *ere*

10. ______________________

For each bold word, write the spelling word that is the opposite.

11. cloudy ______________________

12. far ______________________

Name ______________________ Date ______________

r-Controlled Vowels air, are, ear, ere

hair	wear	care	square	stairs
pear	chair	where	share	bear

Write the spelling word for each clue.

1. It's a fruit. ______________

2. It's an animal. ______________

3. It's a shape. ______________

4. It can be curly or straight. ______________

5. You climb them. ______________

6. You sit on it. ______________

Write the spelling word that completes each sentence.

7. I ______________ about my best friend.

8. I ______________ my books with him.

9. We both like to ______________ baseball caps.

10. I know ______________ he lives.

Name ______________________ Date ______________

r-Controlled Vowels air, are, ear, ere

hair	wear	care	square	stairs
pear	chair	where	share	bear

Write the spelling words for the given spelling patterns.

r-controlled vowel spelled *air*

1. ______________________ **2.** ______________________

3. ______________________

r-controlled vowel spelled *are*

4. ______________________ **5.** ______________________

6. ______________________

r-controlled vowel spelled *ear*

7. ______________________ **8.** ______________________

9. ______________________

r-controlled vowel spelled *ere*

10. ______________________

Name ______________________ Date ______________

Vowel-Consonant-e and Consonant-le Syllables

mistake	shape	apple	useful	table
inside	purple	hope	little	baseball

Write the spelling word that matches each definition.

1. a hard, round fruit ______________________
2. a piece of furniture with a flat top ______________________
3. something done the wrong way ______________________
4. a game played with a bat and ball ______________________
5. circle or square ______________________
6. a color made by mixing blue and red ______________________
7. to want or wish for something ______________________

Write the spelling word that is an antonym of the bold word.

8. **outside** ______________________
9. **big** ______________________
10. **useless** ______________________

Name ______________________________ Date ______________

Vowel-Consonant-e and Consonant-le Syllables

mistake	shape	apple	useful	table
inside	purple	hope	little	baseball

Write the correct spelling words.

One-syllable spelling words with vowel-consonant-*e*

1. ______________ **2.** ______________

Two-syllable spelling words with vowel-consonant-*e*

3. ______________ **4.** ______________

5. ______________ **6.** ______________

Two-syllable spelling words with consonant-*le*

7. ______________ **8.** ______________

9. ______________ **10.** ______________

Write a spelling word with each prefix or suffix.

11. prefix **in-** ______________ **12.** prefix **mis-** ______________

13. suffix **–ful** ______________

Name ______________________________ Date ____________________

Vowel Teams /oi/: oi, oy

joyful	coin	toy	voice	join
boy	noise	boil	enjoy	point

Write a spelling word to complete each sentence.

1. The little ____________________ is learning to walk.

2. He talks in a soft ____________________.

3. He wants a new ____________________ to play with.

4. Please ____________________ to the ball you want.

5. I need another ____________________ to buy the ball.

Write the spelling word that is a synonym of the bold word.

6. happy ____________________

7. sound ____________________

8. link ____________________

9. cook ____________________

10. like ____________________

Name ______________________ Date ______________

Vowel Teams /oi/: oi, oy

joyful	coin	toy	voice	join
boy	noise	boil	enjoy	point

Write the correct spelling words.

Spelling words with vowel team *oi*

1. ______________ **2.** ______________

3. ______________ **4.** ______________

5. ______________ **6.** ______________

One-syllable spelling words with vowel team *oy*

7. ______________ **8.** ______________

Two-syllable spelling words with vowel team *oy*

9. ______________ **10.** ______________

Circle the two spelling words that rhyme.

11. toy voice boy joyful

12. point coin boil join

Name ______________________ Date ______________

Vowel Teams /ou/: ou, ow

now	house	brown	out	town
count	owl	mouth	cow	round

Circle the spelling word that best completes each sentence. Write it on the line.

1. The ______________ gives us fresh milk.

house cow owl

2. She is ______________ and white.

brown now count

3. She walks ______________ into the field.

owl mouth out

4. She chews grass with her ______________.

round mouth town

5. I like the park in my ______________.

round out town

6. My ______________ is close to school.

house owl brown

Name ______________________ Date ______________

Vowel Teams /ou/: ou, ow

now	house	brown	out	town
count	owl	mouth	cow	round

Write the correct spelling words.

3-letter spelling word with vowel team *ou*

1. ______________________

3-letter spelling words with vowel team *ow*

2. ______________________ **3.** ______________________

4. ______________________

4-letter spelling word with vowel team *ow*

5. ______________________

5-letter spelling word with vowel team *ow*

6. ______________________

5-letter spelling words with vowel team *ou*

7. ______________________ **8.** ______________________

9. ______________________ **10.** ______________________

Name ______________________ Date ______________

Vowel Teams /ōō/: oo, ui, ew, ue, u, oe

truth	grew	soon	fruit	June
shoe	new	too	blue	true

Write the spelling word for each clue.

1. It's the name of a month. ______________

2. You wear it on your foot. ______________

3. A liar would not tell you this. ______________

4. This is the color of the sky. ______________

5. It means "also." ______________

6. Pears and apples are this kind of food. ______________

7. It means a short time from now. ______________

Read each word. Then write the spelling word that is an antonym.

8. old ______________

9. false ______________

10. shrunk ______________

Name ______________________________ Date ________________

Vowel Teams /o͞o/: oo, ui, ew, ue, u, oe

truth	grew	soon	fruit	June
shoe	new	too	blue	true

Write the spelling words for the given spelling pattern.

Spelling words with *oo*

1. ________________ **2.** ________________

Spelling word with *ui*

3. ________________

Spelling word with *oe*

4. ________________

Spelling words with *ew*

5. ________________ **6.** ________________

Spelling words with *ue*

7. ________________ **8.** ________________

Spelling words with *u*

9. ________________ **10.** ________________

Name ______________________ Date ______________

Vowel Teams /o͝o/: oo, ou

look	could	stood	would	good
book	shook	foot	should	cook

Circle the spelling word that best completes each sentence. Then write it on the line.

1. Marcus borrowed a ______________ from the library.

foot book look

2. He said it was a ______________ story.

good look cook

3. I ______________ also like to read it.

stood would shook

4. Do you think I ______________ borrow it next?

book stood could

5. The librarian ______________ at the checkout desk.

shook stood should

6. She will help us ______________ for other books to read.

look good cook

Name ______________________ Date ______________

Vowel Teams /o͝o/: oo, ou

look	could	stood	would	good
book	shook	foot	should	cook

Write the correct spelling words.

4-letter spelling words with vowel team *oo*

1. ______________ **2.** ______________

3. ______________ **4.** ______________

5. ______________

5-letter spelling words with vowel team *oo*

6. ______________ **7.** ______________

Spelling words with vowel team *ou*

8. ______________ **9.** ______________

10. ______________

In each row, circle the two spelling words that rhyme.

11. should shook would foot

12. could look foot cook

Name ______________________________ Date ____________________

Vowel Teams /ô/: al, aw, au

small	walk	straw	ball	fault
talk	salt	draw	launch	tall

Write the spelling word that matches each definition.

1. very high ______________

2. to send off into space ______________

3. round object that can be thrown, hit, or kicked __________

4. to make a picture using a pencil, pen, or crayons

____

5. added to food for taste ______________

6. thin tube used to drink liquid ______________

7. reason for a mistake ______________

Read each word. Then write the spelling word that is an antonym.

8. tiny __________________

9. chat __________________

10. stroll __________________

Name ______________________________ Date ____________________

Vowel Teams /ô/: al, aw, au

small	walk	straw	ball	fault
talk	salt	draw	launch	tall

Write the correct spelling words.

Spelling words with vowel team *al*

1. ____________________ **2.** ____________________

3. ____________________ **4.** ____________________

5. ____________________ **6.** ____________________

Spelling words with vowel team *aw*

7. ____________________ **8.** ____________________

Spelling words with vowel team *au*

9. ____________________ **10.** ____________________

Circle the two spelling words that rhyme.

11. launch ball small tall draw salt

Name ______________________ Date ______________

Compound Words

starfish	railroad	moonlight	cowboy	toothbrush
bathroom	birthday	doorknob	snowball	seashell

Write the spelling word for each clue.

1. It's fun to throw in winter. ______________________

2. It has five arms and lives in the ocean.

____

3. It's a crab's home. ______________________

4. It's where you take a shower. ______________________

5. You turn this to enter. ______________________

6. It shines at night. ______________________

7. It's a track for a train. ______________________

8. Your dentist says to use this. ______________________

9. He keeps the herd together. ______________________

10. It's my special day! ______________________

Name ______________________ Date ______________

Compound Words

starfish	railroad	moonlight	cowboy	toothbrush
bathroom	birthday	doorknob	snowball	seashell

Write the spelling words for the given spelling pattern.

Spelling words that end with *ll*

1. ______________ **2.** ______________

Spelling words with *oo*

3. ______________ **4.** ______________

5. ______________ **6.** ______________

Spelling words with *ai* or *ay*

7. ______________ **8.** ______________

Write the spelling word that best completes each sentence.

9. The ranch at the end of the road belongs to a true

______________.

10. I saw a beautiful ______________ at the beach.

Name ______________________ Date ______________

Inflectional Endings with Spelling Changes

swimming	raked	using	hopped	liked
sitting	taking	smiled	running	making

Write the spelling word for each clue.

1. the opposite of **frowned** ______________________

2. faster than walking ______________________

3. how fish get around ______________________

4. gathered leaves into a pile ______________________

5. went in short, quick jumps ______________________

Write the spelling word that best completes each sentence.

6. Dad is ______________________ breakfast.

7. He is ______________________ a lot of pepper.

8. Mom and Brian are ______________________ at the table.

9. Brian is ______________________ another plate.

10. Everyone ______________________ Dad's breakfast.

Name ______________________________ Date ________________

Inflectional Endings with Spelling Changes

swimming	raked	using	hopped	liked
sitting	taking	smiled	running	making

Write the spelling words that match the given rule for forming the past or present tense of the word.

Past tense: double the final consonant and add *-ed*

1. ______________________

Past tense: delete the final *e* and add *-ed*

2. ______________________ **3.** ______________________

4. ______________________

Present tense: Double the final consonant and add *-ing*

5. ______________________ **6.** ______________________

7. ______________________

Present tense: delete the final *e* and add *-ing*

8. ______________________ **9.** ______________________

10. ______________________

Name ______________________________ Date ____________________

Related Root Words

forgot	move	work	add	forgotten
moving	forgetful	addition	worked	movers

Circle the spelling word that best completes the sentence. Then write it on the line.

1. We ______________ hard in class yesterday.

work worked forgot

2. Please ______________ your chairs into a circle.

move movers moving

3. Who can help me with this ______________ problem?

add addition worked

4. Jason ______________ to bring his lunch today.

forgetful forgotten forgot

5. The coach will ______________ Tara and Scott to the team.

forgotten add movers

6. I always make a list because I am ______________.

forgetful worked move

Name ______________________ Date ______________

Related Root Words

forgot	move	work	add	forgotten
moving	forgetful	addition	worked	movers

Write the spelling words formed from the given root word.

work

1. ______________________

add

2. ______________________

forgot

3. ______________________

4. ______________________

move

5. ______________________

6. ______________________

Write the correct spelling words for each clue.

Spelling words used in math

7. ______________________

8. ______________________

Spelling words that begin with *for-*

9. ______________________

10. ______________________

11. ______________________

Name ______________________________ Date ____________________

Irregular Plural Nouns

people	men	shelves	feet	fish
women	teeth	lives	sheep	children

Write the correct spelling word that matches each definition.

1. more than one man ____________________

2. more than one woman ____________________

3. more than one child ____________________

4. more than one person ____________________

Write a spelling word to complete each sentence.

5. There are many striped ____________ in the pond.

6. We saw three ____________ eating grass on the hill.

7. The ____________ in the library hold many books.

8. I wear boots on my ____________ when it snows.

9. A shark has rows of sharp ____________ in its mouth.

10. Our ____________ are safer because of firefighters.

Name ______________________ Date ______________

Irregular Plural Nouns

people	men	shelves	feet	fish
women	teeth	lives	sheep	children

Write the correct spelling words.

Spelling words with two syllables

1. ______________ **2.** ______________

3. ______________

Spelling words with *ee*

4. ______________ **5.** ______________

6. ______________

Spelling words with *v*

7. ______________ **8.** ______________

Spelling words with one vowel

9. ______________ **10.** ______________

Circle the two spelling words that name a group of animals.

11. fish shelves teeth sheep

Name ______________________________ Date ________________

Words with -er or -or Endings

dancer	inventor	teacher	baker	actor
writer	doctor	sailor	farmer	visitor

Write the spelling word for each clue.

1. My job is to help sick people. ________________

2. I work on a ship. ________________

3. I think of and make new kinds of things. ________________

4. My job is to pretend I'm someone else. ________________

5. I grow things and sell them. ________________

6. I help students learn. ________________

7. I perform with music on stage. ________________

8. I make up stories and create books. ________________

9. I cook bread and pastries. ________________

Fill in the boxes for the spelling word *visitor*.

word meaning	**sentence**
visitor	
synonym	**places he or she goes**

Name ______________________ Date ______________

Words with -er or -or Endings

dancer	inventor	teacher	baker	actor
writer	doctor	sailor	farmer	visitor

Write the correct spelling words for the given ending.

Spelling words that end with *-er*

1. ______________ **2.** ______________

3. ______________ **4.** ______________

5. ______________

Spelling words that end with *-or*

6. ______________ **7.** ______________

8. ______________ **9.** ______________

10. ______________

Circle the spelling words that have three syllables.

11. farmer teacher inventor writer

sailor actor doctor visitor

Name ______________________ Date ______________

Comparatives -er, -est

tallest	colder	newer	fastest	slower
faster	slowest	coldest	taller	newest

Circle the spelling word that completes each sentence. Then write it on the line.

1. It is ____________ in January than in June. colder coldest

2. Is January the ________ month of the year? colder coldest

3. Gina has the ______________ bike of all. faster fastest

4. Tam's bike is ______________ than my bike. faster fastest

5. The oak tree is __________ than my house. taller tallest

6. It is the ________ tree in the neighborhood. taller tallest

7. Please wear the __________ shirt you have. newer newest

8. The blue shirt is ________ than the red shirt. newer newest

9. The bus is ______________ than the train. slower slowest

10. Is this the ______________ bus ever? slower slowest

Name ______________________ Date ______________

Comparatives -er, -est

tallest	colder	newer	fastest	slower
faster	slowest	coldest	taller	newest

Write the correct spelling words.

Spelling words that compare two things

1. ______________ **2.** ______________

3. ______________ **4.** ______________

5. ______________

Spelling words that compare more than two things

6. ______________ **7.** ______________

8. ______________ **9.** ______________

10. ______________

Circle the two spelling words that are antonyms of each other.

11. faster newer taller slower

Name ______________________________ Date ________________

Words with -y or -ly Endings

rainy	messy	friendly	happy	slowly
quickly	funny	lucky	neatly	likely

Write a spelling word to complete each sentence.

1. My grandmother thinks a four-leaf clover is ____________.
2. I take an umbrella when the weather is ____________.
3. My best friend tells ____________ jokes.
4. Mom told me to clean my ____________ room.
5. It's important to write ____________ when you complete homework.
6. I'm always ____________ to new students in school.
7. It is very ____________ that our team will win the game.
8. My dog is ____________ when I give him a new toy.

Circle the two spelling words that are antonyms.

9. slowly funny likely quickly
10. friendly neatly messy rainy

Name ______________________ Date ______________

Words with -y or -ly Endings

rainy	messy	friendly	happy	slowly
quickly	funny	lucky	neatly	likely

Write the correct spelling words.

5-letter spelling words that end with *-y*

1. ______________ **2.** ______________

3. ______________ **4.** ______________

5. ______________

6-letter spelling words that end with *-ly*

6. ______________ **7.** ______________

8. ______________

7-letter and 8-letter spelling words that end with *-ly*

9. ______________ **10.** ______________

Circle the spelling words that could be used to describe a person.

11. happy rainy funny friendly

Name ______________________________ Date ____________________

Schwa

again	alone	away	about	awake
ago	alike	above	along	ahead

Circle the spelling word that best completes each sentence. Write it on the line.

1. I went to the museum a few years ______________.

ago about

2. I'd like to visit the museum ______________.

along again

3. I don't want to go to the museum ______________.

alike alone

4. When my brother is ______________, I'll ask him to go.

awake ago

5. My brother and I are a lot ______________.

alike alone

6. We both enjoy learning ______________ airplanes.

ahead about

7. Old planes hang ______________ the museum floor.

above away

Name ______________________ Date ______________

Schwa

again	alone	away	about	awake
ago	alike	above	along	ahead

Write the correct spelling words.

Spelling words with long *o*

1. ______________ **2.** ______________

Spelling words with long *a*

3. ______________ **4.** ______________

Spelling word with long *i*

5. ______________

Spelling words that begin with schwa but do not have a long vowel

6. ______________ **7.** ______________

8. ______________ **9.** ______________

10. ______________

For each bold word, write the spelling word that is an antonym.

11. asleep ______________ **12. below** ______________

Name ________________________ Date ________________

Silent Letters

wrong	gnat	comb	knock	sign
thumb	write	know	climb	knife

Write the spelling word for each definition.

1. You can use it to cut bread. ______________
2. It is a small flying bug. ______________
3. It is a part of your hand. ______________
4. You run it through knots in your hair. ______________
5. You do it with a pen or pencil. ______________
6. It is the opposite of correct. ______________
7. It gives you information. ______________
8. You can use a ladder to do it. ______________
9. You do it to get someone to open a door. ______________
10. You are aware of the facts about something. ______________

Name ______________________ Date ______________

Silent Letters

wrong	gnat	comb	knock	sign
thumb	write	know	climb	knife

Write the correct spelling words.

Spelling words with silent *b*

1. ______________ **2.** ______________

3. ______________

Spelling words with silent *g*

4. ______________ **5.** ______________

Spelling words with silent *k*

6. ______________ **7.** ______________

8. ______________

Spelling words with silent *w*

9. ______________ **10.** ______________

Circle the spelling words that are verbs.

11. climb gnat knife write

Name ______________________________ Date ____________________

Possessives

sun's	houses'	cat's	children's	doctors'
dogs'	mom's	tree's	classes'	boys'

Write a spelling word to complete each sentence.

1. All the ________________ leashes are hanging by the door.

2. My ________________ sister is my Aunt Kay.

3. Are the ________________ offices close to the hospital?

4. This ________________ leaves turn red in the fall.

5. The ________________ light helps plants grow.

6. On our block, all the ________________ doors are red.

7. The author writes ______________ books for kindergartners.

8. My brothers shop in the ________________ clothing department.

9. My ________________ toys are all over the room.

10. In our school, the ________________ starting time is 9:00 a.m.

Name ______________________________ Date ____________________

Possessives

sun's	houses'	cat's	children's	doctors'
dogs'	mom's	tree's	classes'	boys'

Write the correct spelling words.

Singular possessives ending in *'s* (belonging to one)

1. ____________________ **2.** ____________________

3. ____________________ **4.** ____________________

Plural possessives ending in *s'* (belonging to more than one)

5. ____________________ **6.** ____________________

7. ____________________ **8.** ____________________

9. ____________________

Plural possessive ending in *'s* (belonging to more than one)

10. ____________________

Circle possessives that show ownership by a person or people.

11. sun's children's tree's mom's

12. doctors' houses' dogs' boys'

Name ______________________________ Date ____________________

Prefixes un-, re-, dis-

disagree	reread	unpack	distrust	unsafe
reuse	unlock	reheat	dislike	unhappy

Circle the spelling word that best completes each sentence. Write it on the line.

1. I ______________ eating cold noodles.
   distrust   dislike
2. Dad will ______________ the noodles for me.
   reheat   unlock
3. I am ______________ when vacation is over.
   unhappy   unsafe
4. Did you ______________ as soon as you got home?
   reuse   unpack
5. I ______________ that the book is boring.
   disagree   distrust
6. Why don't you try to ______________ the book?
   dislike   reread

Fill in the boxes for the spelling word *unlock*.

meaning	**sentence**
antonym	**things that unlock**

unlock

Name ______________________________ Date ____________________

Prefixes un-, re-, dis-

disagree	reread	unpack	distrust	unsafe
reuse	unlock	reheat	dislike	unhappy

Write the correct spelling words for the given prefix.

Spelling words that begin with *un-*

1. ____________________ **2.** ____________________

3. ____________________ **4.** ____________________

Spelling words that begin with *re-*

5. ____________________ **6.** ____________________

7. ____________________

Spelling words that begin with *dis-*

8. ____________________ **9.** ____________________

10. ____________________

For each row, circle the spelling word that has three syllables.

11. unlock dislike unhappy reread

12. reuse unpack reheat disagree

Name ______________________ Date ______________

Suffixes -ful, -less

painless	careful	spotless	spoonful	speechless
useful	fearless	colorful	priceless	helpful

Write a spelling word for each definition.

1. very valuable ______________
2. having all the shades of the rainbow ______________
3. not afraid of anything ______________
4. easy; causing no stress ______________
5. completely clean; not one spec of dirt ______________
6. so surprised or upset you can't talk ______________
7. trying hard to do something right ______________

Circle the spelling word that best completes each sentence. Then write it on the line.

8. Maya is a ______________ person who always volunteers.

   helpful speechless

9. A pump is ______________ when your bike tire goes flat.

   fearless useful

10. Grandma likes a ______________ of honey in her tea.

    colorful spoonful

Name ______________________ Date ______________

Suffixes -ful, -less

painless	careful	spotless	spoonful	speechless
useful	fearless	colorful	priceless	helpful

Write the correct spelling words for the given suffix.

Spelling words that end with *-ful*

1. ______________ **2.** ______________

3. ______________ **4.** ______________

5. ______________

Spelling words that end with *-less*

6. ______________ **7.** ______________

8. ______________ **9.** ______________

10. ______________

For each word below, write the spelling word that is an antonym.

11. dirty ______________

12. plain ______________

13. scared ______________